"Go and make disciples of all nations, baptizing them in the name of the Father and of the Son and of the Holy Spirit, and teaching them to obey all that I have commanded you" (Matt. 28:19–20).

The Great Commission encompasses the whole task of the church. And here is help for fulfilling that task—the DISCIPLING RESOURCES series. Designed for small-group use, whether Bible study, Sunday school, or fellowship groups, this effective approach is firmly based on biblical principles of disciple building.

Each group member receives his or her own copy of the book, which guides the group through thirteen weekly meetings. Every step of the group- and personal-study process is included, plus biblical material and commentary. Leaders need only facilitate participation. This series is designed to increase knowledge of God's Word, cultivate supportive personal relationships, and stimulate spiritual growth—an adventure in being His disciples.

Titles in this exciting new series:

Available now	Projected
Basic Christian Values	*Being Christ's Church (Ephesians)*
First Steps for New and Used Christians	*Discipling Your Emotions*
	Developing Personal Responsibility
Fruit of the Spirit	*A Life of Fellowship (1 John)*
The Good Life (Rom. 12–16)	

FRUIT OF THE SPIRIT

LARRY RICHARDS
NORM WAKEFIELD

ZONDERVAN PUBLISHING HOUSE
OF THE ZONDERVAN CORPORATION
GRAND RAPIDS, MICHIGAN 49506

FRUIT OF THE SPIRIT
© 1981 by The Zondervan Corporation

Library of Congress Cataloging in Publication Data

Richards, Lawrence O .
    Fruit of the Spirit.

    (Discipling resources)
    1. Gifts, Spiritual—Study and teaching. 2. Bible. N.T. Galatians V, 22—Study. I. Wakefield, Norm, joint author. II. Title.
III. Series.

BT767.3.R53   234'.12   80-27917
ISBN 0-310-43401-7

CONTENTS

CHOOSING
THE FRUITFUL LIFE 1

Paul outlines
important ways
the Spirit
expresses Himself
in our lives.
Let's investigate
how He relates to
you and me.

GATHER

in groups of six or
seven to play the game
of *Bidding War.*

On this page you see a list of nine kinds of "fruit of the Spirit." Imagine that you have $100. You are to use this money to bid on the fruit or fruits that you want for yourself. You may split your money to bid on two or more, or you may bid on just one.

When you have decided, bid against the others in your group for the fruit you have chosen. You may change your planned bids as you wish at any time during the war. Try to select and win at least one of the fruit. But be sure it or they are fruit you really want.

When one of the group has made a winning bid, enter his or her name by the fruit purchased. Continue the bidding war until everyone has had an opportunity to buy at least one item on the list.

When you've finished the bidding war game, turn the page and continue.

LOVE _____

JOY _____

PEACE _____

PATIENCE _____

KINDNESS _____

GOODNESS _____

FAITHFULNESS _____

GENTLENESS _____

SELF-CONTROL _____

Discuss
in your group
of six or eight.

1 Why did you bid on the fruit you purchased?

2 Did you bid on the fruit because you have it in your life now . . . or because you want it?

3 In what situations do you want to experience this fruit?

4 When have you seen this quality expressed in the life of someone else?

READ
this Bible passage.
Answer the questions
on the next page.

So I say, live by the Spirit, and you will not gratify the desires of the sinful nature. For the sinful nature desires what is contrary to the Spirit, and the Spirit what is contrary to the sinful nature. They are in conflict with each other, so that you do not do what you want. But if you are led by the Spirit, you are not under law.

The acts of the sinful nature are obvious: sexual immorality, impurity and debauchery; idolatry and witchcraft; hatred, discord, jealousy, fits of rage, selfish ambition, dissentions, factions and envy; drunkenness, orgies, and the like. I warn you, as I did before, that those who live like this will not inherit the kingdom of God.

But the fruit of the Spirit is love, joy, peace, patience, kindness, goodness, faithfulness, gentleness, and self-control. Against such things there is no law. Those who belong to Christ Jesus have crucified the sinful nature with its passions and desires. Since we live by the Spirit, let us keep in step with the Spirit. Let us not become conceited, provoking and envying each other.

Galatians 5:16–26

SELECT

your answer to
the following questions.

_____ **1** The main emphasis in this passage is on (a) my relationship with the Spirit of God, (b) not practicing sinful acts, (c) acting like a Christian, (d) how to inherit the kingdom of God.

_____ **2** According to this passage the evidence of spirituality is (a) supernatural miracles in my life, (b) a life full of conflict and frustration, (c) a life free of conflict, (d) the expression of specific character qualities.

_____ **3** The passage teaches that the Spirit (a) frees me from legalism, (b) frees me from subjectivism,(c) frees me from sinful behavior, (d) all of the above.

_____ **4** According to this passage, Christian living is based on (a) what I do, (b) what the Spirit does in me, (c) a daily, cooperative relationship between the Spirit and me, (d) none of the above.

_____ **5** The nine-fold fruit of the Spirit (a) is the work of God's grace, (b) is based on our keeping the laws of God, (c) is an ideal too unrealistic to achieve, (d) is something we'll receive in heaven.

COMPARE

your answers
with those of others
in your group.

A Word from Larry

It's exciting to realize that so many life-enriching blessings are to flow from our relationship with God. Jesus' gift of the Holy Spirit to us is a gift which promises freedom from all that we hate in ourselves and growth of all those traits of character that we admire so much in others. Growth in our relationship with God is growth toward being that loving, joyful, peace-filled, patient, kind, good, faithful, gentle, and self-controlled person we have always wanted to be.

Our Bible passage contains not only this promise, but also an invitation. "Live by the Spirit. . . . Be led by the Spirit. . . . Keep in step with the Spirit." *We are to appropriate and to act on the promises of God.*

That's what this discipleship resource course on the Fruit of the Spirit is about. Exploring together how we can act in faith, responding to the Spirit as He calls us to vital life in Him. As we explore together each of the fruit listed in Galatians 5, we will actually take steps of faith together. We will trust the Spirit to work in our lives and through us as we encourage and help each other to build a loving, joyful, peaceful and patient lifestyle—in Him.

THIS WEEK

Discipleship is more than "learning." It involves putting what we learn into daily practice. You have two means to practice daily the truths explored in this study.

First, each study includes a daily diary. You can jot down your meditation notes and make notes on what God is teaching you from the Scriptures. Also record ways that you have put the truths of the Word into daily practice.

Second, each of you will be teamed with another person taking this study. Your responsibility will be (1) to pray for your partner daily and (2) to meet with your partner or talk with him or her by phone at least once during the week. Many will want to meet for coffee or lunch. When you are together, share what you have recorded in your diary and your daily experiences. And share prayer requests. Also, do make praying together part of your meeting.

Here is space to jot down your partner's name, address, and phone number, and your weekly appointment time. Do take time *now* to pair off in partnership teams.

My partner's name _____

Partner's address _____

Partner's phone _____

Appointment time _____

Appointment place _____

Bible passage for meditation this week: John 14–16. Read this passage daily, and daily respond to this question: What do I see here about my own relationship with the Holy Spirit?

STUDY JOHN 14–16

DAY 1

DAY 2

DAY 3

DAY 4

DAY 5

DAY 6

REACHING OUT

Jesus said,
"Love one another,
as I have loved you."
His words
have spoken to men
and women
through the centuries.
What will
they say to you
and me?

READ
this letter.

Dear Craig,

Greetings in our Lord. I keep hearing such positive reports about how God is using you that I can hardly wait to visit you! I want to hear first hand. You do have such a gracious way with folks that they often come to you for spiritual help.

Craig, the main reason I have for writing this is Ray Elliot. When you told me eighteen months ago he had embezzled fifty thousand dollars from you, I was astonished. As you know, he was sent to the Bardoor Correction Farm here in Sloan County. I started visiting him regularly, and God graciously used this to bring a remarkable transformation in his life. His growth has been so genuine that I look forward to being with him. He has spent some weekends with our family, and Ella and the children value his visits.

Craig, I'm writing to ask you to consider something. Ray will be released in a couple weeks, and he'll need employment. I wish you'd take him back and give him a job with your firm. I believe he could be very useful to you at this point in your company's growth. However, it will be important for you to accept him as a brother, not just an employee.

Imagine this letter
was sent to you.
What might your feelings
about Ray Elliot be?
Jot them down here:

Would you hire him back?
____ Yes   ____ No

Why, or why not?

I was reflecting the other day on how God used me in your life to establish your company. You once told me I was the most influential Christian in your life. From that perspective, I suppose I could pressure you to take Ray back as a favor to me. But my prayer is that you will want to take him back out of love.

I look forward to your reply.

In Christ's love,

Hank

WRITE

Now write
a letter to Hank,
telling him of
your decision.

Dear Hank,

_____

_____

_____

_____

_____

_____

_____

_____

_____

_____

_____

_____

_____

Craig

READ

Here is a Bible passage that parallels Hank's letter.

I always thank my God as I remember you in my prayers, because I hear about your faith in the Lord Jesus and your love for all the saints. I pray that you may be active in sharing your faith, so that you will have a full understanding of every good thing we have in Christ. Your love has given me great joy and encouragement, because you, brother, have refreshed the hearts of the saints.

Therefore, although in Christ I could be bold and order you to do what you ought to do, yet I appeal to you on the basis of love. I then, as Paul—an old man and now also a prisoner of Christ Jesus—I appeal to you for my son Onesimus, who became my son while I was in chains. Formerly he was useless to you, but now he has become useful both to you and to me.

I am sending him—who is my very heart—back to you. I would have liked to keep him with me so that he could take your place in helping me while I am in chains for the gospel. But I did not want to do anything without your consent, so that any favor you do will be spontaneous and not forced. Perhaps the reason he was separated from you for a little while was that you might have him back for good—no longer as a slave, but better than a slave, as a dear brother. He is very dear to me but even dearer to you, both as a man and as a brother in the Lord.

So, if you consider me a partner, welcome him as you would welcome me. If he has done any wrong or owes you anything, charge it to me.

Philemon 4-18

DISCUSS

in groups
of six.

1 Why do you think Paul was unwilling to command "what you ought to do" and instead appealed "on the basis of love"?

2 What would it require on Philemon's part to accept Onesimus back "as a brother"?

3 How would Onesimus be able to tell if Philemon's acceptance of him was out of duty or love? What specific ways would such a love be expressed and experienced?

4 Why does this kind of love require the working (fruit) of the Holy Spirit?

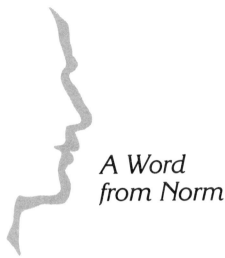

A Word from Norm

Love is a word of *relationship.* To say that God is love is to affirm the fact that God yearns to enter into close and personal relationship with you and me, that He is eager to grow into our lives—to enrich, to help, and to liberate us.

God's love liberates us by freeing us to enter loving relationships with others around us.

Some kinds of relationships are so rewarding that they do not seem to require a liberating act of God. We care for our children spontaneously. We enjoy the company of friends who enjoy ours. Of course there are times of irritation or alienation. But usually we find it's not too difficult to forgive those who love us as we love them.

But Scripture presents God as a Person who loves even His enemies! "God shows his love for us," Romans 5 says, "in that while we were yet sinners Christ died for us" (v. 8 RSV). And Jesus told his disciples, "You have heard it said, 'You shall love your neighbor and hate your enemy.' But I say to you, Love your enemies and pray for those who persecute you, so that you may be sons of your Father who is in heaven; for he makes his sun to rise on the evil and on the good, and sends rain on the just and on the unjust" (Matt. 5:43 RSV).

This kind of love is truly supernatural. It is more than a reflection of God's love. It *is* God's love. God's love first given to us, and then given *through* us.

Living in the power of the Holy Spirit involves the living expression of God's own love to those around us who may even have made themselves our enemies.

What is exciting is God's promise that such love is a fruit that grows in us through the work of the Holy Spirit in us. Because of God's promise, we are able to act in love. We are able to reach out in loving, caring ways, to touch even those we have not liked in the past. As we reach out, God works in our lives to help us begin to care for them. And God works in our lives to help the other person experience a love that is His own.

We cannot promise or even expect an immediate change in a relationship as we begin to love. But as we continue to pray that God will bear his fruit of love in our lives, *we* will begin to change.

And with time, God's love will melt even the hardest heart.

THIS WEEK

Jot down the name of someone you come into contact with regularly, whom you find very difficult to love.

_____

LOVE

How might you meaningfully express love toward that person? What to him or her might be an indication of a loving attitude?

_____

_____

_____

_____

SHARE

with your partner the name of the person you wrote down. Talk with him or her about that relationship. Why do you find it difficult to love the person you identified? How might love be expressed? What would you like God to do in your life as you follow through by showing love to that individual this week?

Pray together about the coming week and your relationships with the individuals you each named.

Record in your journal pages items about your contact with the individual you named. Pray daily for him or her. And for meditation read one chapter from 1 John each day.

JOURNAL

STUDY 1 JOHN 3

DAY 1

DAY 2

DAY 3

DAY 4

DAY 5

DAY 6

ON MY WAY 3 REJOICING

How can a person
experience joy
when circumstances
are rough?
Christ has an answer
to that question.
Let's see
what He says.

WRITE
In a sentence or two
describe several situations
in which you experienced joy.

_____

_____

_____

_____

_____

_____

What is your definition of joy?

_____

_____

_____

_____

_____

_____

_____

How do you think Jesus would define joy?

_____

_____

_____

_____

_____

_____

_____

IMAGINE

you are interviewing
Jesus. What situations
in His life would He mention
as bringing Him joy?

_____

_____

_____

_____

_____

_____

_____

_____

LOOK UP

with your partner
the following
Bible verses and
jot down
what you feel
they teach about
joy.

DISCUSS

together
in the group how
what you
have discovered
in these verses
compares
with the two
definitions of joy
written on
the previous page.

Luke 10:17-21 _____

_____

Luke 24:52 _____

_____

John 15:9-11 _____

_____

John 16:21-24 _____

_____

John 17:13 _____

_____

Acts 5:41 _____

_____

Hebrews 12:2 _____

_____

A Word from Norm

In what settings does joy typically express itself? Can I find help in knowing what activities, settings, or actions produce a joyful life?

The Scripture gives us insight that helps to answer these questions. For the words "joy" and "rejoicing" appear often in the Bible. They are used over and over again and are one evidence of the Spirit's transforming work in a believer's life.

Joy is frequently linked in the Bible to our relationships with others. Paul tells of his relationship with the Thessalonian believers and calls them his joy and hope of rejoicing (1 Thess. 2:19–20). This is especially true of relationships in which we are seeking to help others grow. Concern for the well-being of others and indications of their growth are a rich source of joy.

Joy also flows from a loving relationship with our Heavenly Father. Jesus speaks of obedient love in John 15 and explains with these words: "I have told you this so that my joy may be in you and that your joy may be full" (v. 11).

Our relationships with our fellow Christians are a significant factor in knowing joy. Can you think of times when your relationship with someone special was damaged through anger or hurt or misunderstanding or neglect? Didn't you find that something vital was missing . . . that joy was drained away by the damaged relationship?

This suggests that we are wise to prize relationships with our brothers and sisters and to keep relationships strong and healthy.

In Scripture, joy is also linked with ministry to others—contributing to another's life. Paul summarizes this when he reports in 1 Thessalonians 3 that "Now we really live, since you are standing firm in the Lord. How can we thank God enough for all the joy we have in the presence of our God because of you?" (v. 8).

Paul had invested himself in the lives of these people. He had given of himself sacrificially. As he observed them grow into the reality of knowing Christ personally, Paul experienced great joy.

Jesus knew this same joy. He spent Himself freely for others. At times when his disciples urged Him to eat and refresh Himself, Jesus would reply "I have food to eat that you know nothing about. . . . My food . . . is to do the will of him who sent me and to finish his work" (John 4:32, 34). Later the Gospels speak of the joy set before Jesus in enduring the cross . . . and Hebrews restates this theme (Heb. 12:2). Jesus knew joy in self-giving, so that through His effort you and I might live transformed lives, knowing God now and for eternity.

Joy is also connected with challenge. Whenever we discover that God is allowing our lives to be stretched, tested, or enriched, we can experience that spirit of rejoicing. The disciples found that even when physically attacked or verbally abused for Christ's sake, a deep inner joy sprung up to accompany them. The knowledge that God's purposes were being fulfilled in their lives was what made them joyful. As Acts reports, "The apostles left the Sanhedrin, rejoicing because they had been counted worthy of suffering disgrace for the Name" (Acts 5:41).

We too can find deepening joy in seeing God's purposes accomplished and in fitting into our place in His plan.

REACT
to the article
by completing
each sentence.

1 I would experience more joy in my relationship with Jesus if

_____

_____

2 One specific way that I could have deeper joy with my Christian friends would be by

_____

3 Paul found joy in a prison cell. I expect to find joy in _____

_____

_____

TALK OVER
with the group
or by partners.

Share your answers to each question. Why did you answer as you did?

THIS WEEK

Each day this week read one of the verses or short passages listed on page 30. Meditate on the verse and pray that God will build His joy into your life.

Don't forget to pray daily for your partner and to meet him or her at least once this week to share and pray together.

You may want to continue reaching out in love to the individual you ministered to last week. But also see if there are ways that you can contribute to the life of your partner.

Finally, before you write in your journal each day, reread Norm's brief article, and each day circle a different sentence or phrase that seems particularly meaningful to you.

STUDY PHILIPPIANS 3

DAY 1

DAY 2

DAY 3

DAY 4

DAY 5

DAY 6

35

SHALOM

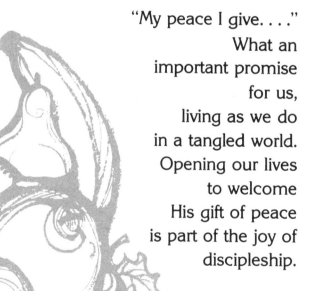

"My peace I give. . . ."
What an
important promise
for us,
living as we do
in a tangled world.
Opening our lives
to welcome
His gift of peace
is part of the joy of
discipleship.

THE SEARCH

I LOOKED FOR PEACE OUTSIDE MY HOUSE BUT ALL I FOUND WERE STRIKES AND RECESSION AND RUSSIAN TROOPS IN CUBA AND CUBAN TROOPS IN AFRICA AND NUCLEAR-PLANT ACCIDENTS AND THE DOLLAR LOSING VALUE AND CRIME AND PORNOGRAPHY AND DRUGS IN GRADE SCHOOLS. I DECIDED TO STAY INSIDE.

I LOOKED FOR PEACE INSIDE MY HOUSE BUT ALL I HEARD WAS TV AND MY KIDS WHINING AND MY WIFE YELLING AT ME TO GO OUT AND WORK AND THE PHONE RINGING AND BILLS AND ONE BATHROOM FOR FIVE PEOPLE. SO I DECIDED TO GO TO THE BASEMENT.

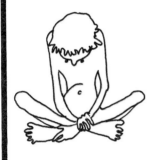

I SAT IN THE BASEMENT AND LOOKED FOR PEACE BY CONTEMPLATING MY NAVEL. BUT ALL I COULD THINK ABOUT WAS WHY MY PARENTS DIDN'T LOVE ME, AND MY ULCERS AND HOW I FAILED ON MY LAST JOB AND HOW I WANTED TO BE A WRITER BUT GOT MARRIED AND HOW I'M GETTING OLD. SO I STAYED IN THE BASEMENT.

WHERE ELSE IS THERE TO LOOK?

READ
this psalm.

The LORD is my shepherd, I shall lack nothing.
  He makes me lie down in green pastures,
he leads me beside quiet waters,
  he restores my soul.
He guides me in paths of righteousness
  for his name's sake.
Even though I walk
  through the valley of the shadow of death,
I will fear no evil,
  for you are with me;
your rod and your staff,
  they comfort me.

You prepare a table before me
  in the presence of my enemies.
You anoint my head with oil;
  my cup overflows.
Surely goodness and love will follow me
  all the days of my life,
and I will dwell in the house of the LORD
  forever.

Psalm 23

RESPOND
to the cartoon
and psalm.

_____

_____

_____

_____

_____

_____

_____

What is the
critical difference
between
the views expressed
by the cartoon
character
and the psalmist?

_____

_____

_____

_____

_____

_____

_____

_____

_____

WRITE

Identify
a tense situation
in your own life now.
Describe here
some characteristics
of the situation.

SHARE

with three
other persons.

_____

_____

_____

_____

_____

_____

_____

_____

_____

_____

_____

_____

_____

_____

_____

_____

_____

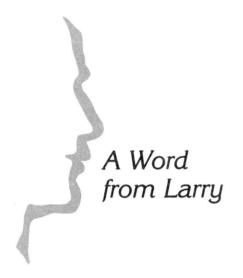

A Word from Larry

The word "peace" occurs often in the New Testament. It's found in every book except 1 John. But roots of the biblical concept of "peace" are Old Testament.

There we are introduced to *shalom,* a term that speaks of "wholeness, completeness." In Joshua the word describes an *uncut* stone (Joshua 8:31); in the little Book of Ruth it describes *full* wages (Ruth 2:12 KJV). In Hebrew thought *shalom* affirms well-being, in the widest sense of that word.

Typically the world views "peace" as the absence of war or tension. Men search for peace by changing the circumstances of their lives. But Jesus, who promises His followers peace, has a different concept.

"Peace I leave with you," Jesus promised. "My peace I give you. I do not give to you as the world gives. Do not let your hearts be troubled and do not be afraid" (John 14:27).

Jesus, who knew rejection, was possessed by peace. Jesus, who knew opposition, remained whole in spite of pressures. Jesus, who knew deep weariness, remained unshattered. Even the active hatred of men for which he came to earth to give His life did not shake His composure or His confidence.

In the same context as that in which He promised peace Jesus prophesied a difficult life for His disciples. "If the world hates you," Jesus taught, "keep in mind that it hated me first. If you belonged to the world, it would love you as its own. As it is, you do not belong to the world, but I have chosen you out of the world. That is why the world hates you. Remember the words I spoke to you: 'No servant is greater than his master.' If they persecuted me, they will persecute you also. If they obeyed my teaching, they will obey yours also. They will treat you this way because of my name, for they do not know the One who sent me" (John 15:18-21).

Notice that Jesus expects his followers to know external kinds of tension. Antagonism, even persecutions, are not to be unexpected. And like other men, we live as members of a twisted society, subject to inflation and crime and all the ills that mar our culture.

What then is the secret of the peace that Jesus promised us? What is the secret of what Jesus called "my" peace, in contrast with the kind of peace provided by the world?

We see the answer in His prophetic warning. Peace —a wholeness, a completeness, a true inner well-being—is found in our personal relationship with God . . . a relationship defined in Jesus' warning in John 15.

We do not belong to the world, but we belong to God. Because the whole life of the unbeliever is oriented to his experience in the material universe, circumstances can shatter his sense of security. Our life is oriented to God. No circumstances can shake Him or change Him, or threaten the certainty that "I am His, and He is mine. Forever."

We have been chosen by Jesus. Our relationship to God is no accident. His own active seeking of us is at the root of our relationship. It is because we know we are loved; we know with certainty that God *is* for us, that the foundation of our peace remains secure.

We share Jesus' experiences in the world. Some promote the notion that God does (or should) protect His children against all disappointments and strains. But Jesus came to be God's servant and to pay the price to communicate the love and sufficiency of God. We are now servants too. And we are not to expect any life different from that of our Master. Because we share in His struggles, we must find a source of peace that gives His peace. A peace that is found in wholeness—not in escape from the tensions of life in the world.

Thus the word *shalom* has deep meaning and a precious promise for us. Shalom is a peace that exists in spite of circumstances. Shalom is a peace that exists because we find our wholeness, and our security, in our relationship with God.

The psalmist found peace even walking "in the valley of the shadow of death." We can find our peace, in our extremities, just where he found it.

"I will fear no evil, for you are with me."

MEDITATE
Read through
this exploration of "peace"
again thoughtfully.
As you reread, circle
the *three* thoughts or phrases
that are most meaningful to you
in view of the personal
"pressure" situation you wrote down
a few minutes ago.

WRITE OUT

your own psalm,
telling God of your
confidence in Him
in the situation
you described
earlier.

_____

_____

_____

_____

_____

_____

_____

_____

_____

_____

_____

_____

_____

_____

SHARE

Then with the
whole group together,
share your psalm
one person at
a time . . . and tell what
it expresses of your situation.

And pray.

THIS WEEK

Meditate on this week's scripture passage and what it suggests about peace. How would it help in the tense situation you are presently facing? What action(s) do you need to take according to the verses? Jot down your thoughts in your journal.

STUDY MATTHEW 11:28–29

DAY 1

DAY 2

DAY 3

DAY 4

DAY 5

DAY 6

ENCOURAGE 5

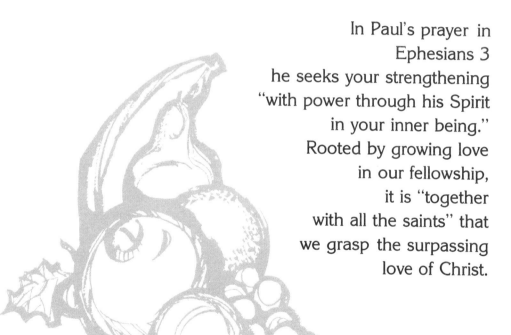

In Paul's prayer in
Ephesians 3
he seeks your strengthening
"with power through his Spirit
in your inner being."
Rooted by growing love
in our fellowship,
it is "together
with all the saints" that
we grasp the surpassing
love of Christ.

ENCOURAGEMENT
reflecting, *sharing,* affirming,
stimulating, reporting, praying

Hebrews urges us not to give up meeting together, but to assemble to "encourage one another." In our gatherings we are to consider "how we may spur one another on toward love and good deeds" (Heb. 10:24–25).

Being together simply for encouragement, not even to explore new content, is a vital part of God's discipling process.

Because encouragement is so important, three of your meetings together focus on deepening relationships and spurring one another on toward deeper love and greater commitment to good deeds.

What does encouragement involve? Many things. Reflecting together. Sharing from our lives and experiences. Affirming one another. Stimulating through interest and accountability. Reporting what God has been doing in our lives. Praying together. All these things are elements of encouraging.

And the focus for this Encouragement session?

Sharing.

CIRCLE

Which of these three fruit
of the Spirit is most
important to you
personally?

Love
Joy
Peace

REVIEW

1-7 **8-15** **16-21**

your experience
of or lack of
the fruit
you just selected as
"most important
to you personally."

What experiences
in your life have
helped make you
especially sensitive
to the importance
of this fruit?

Record
your life experiences
at different ages
using the time line
on these pages.
Take up to
15 minutes.

22-30   31-40   41-45   46-now

SHARE

and record.

Let two or three
of your group
share with the others
their time lines.
As each shares,
jot down
notes that will help
you know and pray
for him or her.

name

name

name

PRAY

Use the last five or ten minutes of your time together for prayer.

But focus your prayer. Spend the first minute or two *listening.* What has God shown you as the others shared? What special needs, or special strengths?

Then pray aloud together, expecting the Spirit to guide you as you ask the Lord to strengthen your brother or sister, and praise God for what He has been doing in each life.

THIS WEEK

This week concentrate on encouraging your partner . . . and yourself.

Meet at some time during the week with your partner and share your time lines. Listen sensitively for what God is saying through your lives. Then pray together, asking God to help you pray wisely and praise joyfully for what He is doing in each other.

This week focus your journal entries on God's action in your life. How is His presence shown? How are your responses to Him more godly than they used to be? Find daily evidence of His working in you, and praise the Lord daily for each discovery.

Here's a theme verse to meditate on. "He who began a good work in you will carry it on to completion until the day of Jesus Christ" (Phil. 1:6).

STUDY PSALM 111

DAY 1

DAY 2

DAY 3

DAY 4

DAY 5

DAY 6

YOU HAVE NEED OF PATIENCE 6

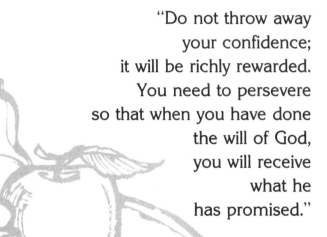

"Do not throw away
your confidence;
it will be richly rewarded.
You need to persevere
so that when you have done
the will of God,
you will receive
what he
has promised."

Hebrews 10:36

CHECK LIST

What are things that tend to make you feel frustrated and impatient? Check off things that really bother you.

_____ waiting in checkout line
_____ a meal is late
_____ slow traffic
_____ slow co-workers
_____ getting children to bed
_____ a fire won't light
_____ putting a complicated toy together
_____ your team loses
_____ spouse makes a mistake
_____ subordinate curses
_____ bill is in error
_____ poor utility service
_____ waiting in doctor's office
_____ broken equipment
_____ people won't return call
_____ junk mail
_____ door-to-door salespersons
_____ TV advertisements
_____ lack of money
_____ lack of time
_____ rising prices
_____ failure of others to respond
_____ people won't listen
_____ your efforts not appreciated
_____ spouse late to meet you
_____ car won't start
_____ boss won't accept ideas
_____ someone breaks promise

What three things (from list or others) make you the *most* impatient? Write them below.

1 _____

2 _____

3 _____

PERSPECTIVE

Biblically, the issue of patience does not
focus on our frustrations or our feelings.
The issue of patience deals with attitudes
and actions.

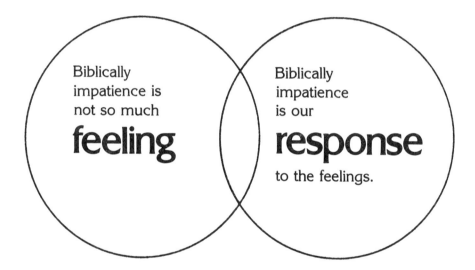

Biblically
impatience is
not so much
feeling

Biblically
impatience
is our
response
to the feelings.

READ
this quote.

Years ago I used to notice the differences among motormen on the Indiana Avenue streetcar line in Chicago—a street often blocked by badly parked cars and huge trailer trucks maneuvering in everybody's way. Some motormen would get steamed up with rage, clang their bells and shout at the drivers. At the end of the day they must have been nervous wrecks, jittery and hypertensive, a menace to their wives and children.

Other motormen, however, could sit and wait for minutes without impatience, calmly whistling a tune, cleaning their fingernails, writing their reports. In other words, confronted with the same objective situation, some motormen lived a hellish life of anger and nervous tension; other motormen had a nice, relaxing job, with plenty of time for rest.*

*Samuel I. Hayakawa, *Symbol, Status, and Personality* (New York: Harcourt Brace Jovanovich, 1963).

DISCUSS
the following.
You may agree,
or disagree.

1 No patience was needed by the second motorman. He didn't care!

2 Perhaps patience means to cope in a positive way with what upsets others.

3 Since neither motorman could control what was happening on his street, the only reasonable response was to make the best of a bad situation.

4 I am (sure/not sure) the second motorman's reaction was godly, because . . .

SHARE
in groups
of five or six.

1 Tell the others the three things you listed which
   make you *most* impatient. How are they like or
   unlike the situation of the two motormen?

2 How do you tend to react in these situations?

A Word from Larry

In a moment you'll share insights from several Scriptures that deal with the subject of patience. Here is a little background that may help.

In the roots of the original language the Greeks saw a sense of resignation. Yet this need not be abandonment or hopelessness. In fact, "patience" might express an unswerving commitment to persevere in spite of discouraging circumstances. In Scripture God is seen as Sovereign Lord, in charge of the events of our lives. Patience, as commitment or perseverence, is an expression of trust in God.

Patience is particularly seen as an attribute of God, who endures man's sinfulness and rebellion, and yet remains committed to show us mercy. Paul, who saw himself as "chief of sinners," thought of his conversion as a display of Christ's "perfect patience" for an example to those who were to believe in Him for eternal life (1 Tim. 1:15-16).

Patience, then, is an active quality. Because we are deeply concerned about others as Jesus' people, we reach out to share with them, even when rebuffed by circumstances or individuals. "Love is patient," Paul says (1 Cor. 13:4), and in this saying shows us a character trait that is translated by God's Spirit in us to become a way of life.

Patience is a commitment to persevere.

Patience is unswerving trust in God.

Patience is Godlike active concern for the well-being of others.

Patience is reaching out to share and to care even when rebuffed.

Patience is both the character and the way of life that Jesus holds out to us as His disciples.

LISTEN

for God's voice.

Read the following verses
from Scripture.
Which most powerfully
touches your life now?

"We want each of you to show this same diligence to the very end, in order to make your hope sure. We do not want you to become lazy, but to imitate those who through faith and patience inherit what has been promised."

Hebrews 6:11–12

You have need to persevere so that when you have done the will of God, you will receive the promise.

Hebrews 10:36

Be patient, then, brothers, until the Lord's coming. . . . Be patient, and stand firm, because the Lord's coming is near. . . . Brothers, as an example of patience in the face of suffering, take the prophets who spoke in the name of the Lord. As you know we consider them blessed who have persevered. You have heard of Job's perseverance and have seen what the Lord finally brought about. The Lord is full of compassion and mercy.

James 5:7–11

Preach the Word; be prepared in season and out of season; correct, rebuke, encourage—with great patience and careful instruction. . . . Keep your head in all situations, endure hardship, do the work of an evangelist, discharge all the duties of your ministry.

2 Timothy 4:2, 5

CONCLUDE

your group time
together by sharing
how God is speaking
to each of you
through His Word.
And take time
to pray together.

MEDITATION
from Norm
to read during
this week.

The Burr Under the Saddle

Before I married I thought I was patient. After I married I discovered my patience had never been tested! Actually, I've been glad for the test. Developing patience has been a great blessing. And in the process I learned much of the dangers of impatience.

Impatience is a great thief of God's joy. It erodes the rejoicing spirit, leaving us frustrated and irritable. Why then do we give in to a spirit of impatience? What makes us fuss and fidget when things don't go our way?

Unrealistic expectations. Mother expects her child to pick up the glass without spilling the milk. When the child upsets the glass, mom may fume. But young children may not have developed necessary muscle control. It's realistic to expect children to spill.

Often Christians have unrealistic expectations aimed at God. "I've prayed! Why doesn't God do something!" Unfortunately some Christian leaders portray God as a Heavenly Genie. "If you only have faith," they say, "God *must* do as you wish." But Scripture shows us that God promises to deliver us *through* our ordeals, not necessarily from them. It is realistic to bring our cries of need to God. But it is then realistic to expect our Heavenly Father to act according to His own wise plan for our lives. To recognize God as Lord and put aside our unrealistic expectations is one source of godly patience.

Immediacy. This is another root of impatience. We are more likely to be impatient with people if we expect to achieve goals immediately rather than through a process. The writer of Hebrews seems to have this in mind when he says, "You have need of endurance, so that when you have done the will of God, you may receive what was promised" (10:36). God is deeply concerned about leading us through a process through which we become mature sons and daughters. We need to learn that often results do not immediately follow action.

How are these two sources of impatience likely to creep into our experience?

We may expect people or God to act according to *our* time schedule. My wife knows I want breakfast at 7:06. It better be ready! Or, I've told God I've waited long enough for my husband to change. God, get busy!

We may have unrealistic values. God should act to punish the evil ones, now. When injustice becomes personal, our impatience increases. We think, It isn't fair! God, why do you permit it?

We may have unrealistic expectations about our relationships. My wife is supposed to submit. It irritates me when she doesn't. Or, Sam is O.K., but he's not my type. We may then become impatient when we have to deal with other people.

And we may even have unrealistic expectations of ourselves. I become impatient when I don't start that diet. Or, I don't follow through on the plan I said I was committed to. False standards of performance may lead us to self-disgust or condemnation.

How can we build patience in spite of the pressures on us to be impatient people? Here are two positive suggestions you may want to follow up on this week. Record these experiences in your journal.

1 Try not to filter God through our human perspective. We can grow in patience as we *consciously seek to evaluate our experiences from God's point of view.* This is why it's so important to entrust ourselves and each day to the Lord. His Spirit will direct us and reshape our perspectives.

2 Try to avoid false time schedules. God is not in a hurry. He allows years for growth; not seconds, minutes, hours, or days. I can discover a more relaxed lifestyle and deepen my patience when I set aside unrealistic pressures from *time* and seek to fall in step with the Spirit.

THIS WEEK

As you keep your journal be sure to find time to share what God is teaching you with your partner. A lunch or other time together is good. A phone call will do.

STUDY MATTHEW 24:36-51

DAY 1

DAY 2

DAY 3

DAY 4

DAY 5

DAY 6

71

7 PUT ON KINDNESS

This is Paul's
exhortation to us
as God's chosen ones
(Col. 3:12 KJV).
What "kindness"
means as an expression
of God's love in us
is the theme
of this
discipleship study.

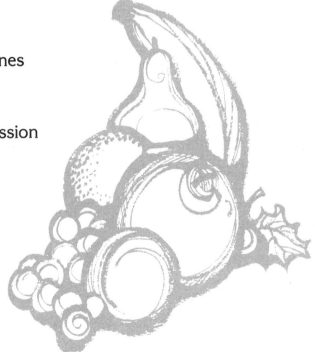

LET'S APPROACH
our study of *kindness*
by thinking first of the idea
of "holy" or "upright."

Represent the impression most people
have of an upright or holy person by
drawing in the mouth of the face on
the left.

Let the mouth you draw reflect the idea
of holiness or uprightness that most
people have.

Show your picture to the others, and
discuss the questions below.

1 Why did you draw the mouth as you did? _____

_____

2 Have you known many people like the one you drew?

_____

3 Would you like this person for a friend? Why, or why not?

_____

_____

BIBLE BACKGROUND

The Greek word translated "kindness" in Galatians originally carried the notion of usefulness. In time the expanded concept of moral excellence was added. Thus it became one of the main words in Greek which denotes *goodness.*

A person who possessed this kind of goodness had a capacity to show kindness to everyone; a capacity which flowed from a genuine goodness of heart.

It was this genuine kindness, flowing from moral excellence, that is reflected in the New Testament idea of *uprightness.*

All too often in our society we have come to think of "goodness" as an austere, impersonal or distant "holiness" that cuts one off from others. In the Bible the opposite is true. Real uprightness, true goodness, is expressed in active kindness to others. No wonder the Bible says that "when the kindness and love of God our Savior appeared, he saved us" (Titus 3:4).

The Spirit of God produces this same kind of active kindness/love in the men and women God is now making holy.

The Bible portrays both Ruth and Boaz, of the Old Testament, as upright persons. In someone else's field Ruth might have been harmed as she gathered grain dropped by the harvesters (Ruth 2:22). But not in Boaz's. And Ruth, though a foreigner, had already won the reputation of a "noble woman" (Ruth 3:11).

READ

Underline attitudes and actions which
show kindness.   Discuss what you discern
about kindness from this biblical account.

Just then Boaz arrived from Bethlehem and greeted the harvesters, "The
LORD be with you!"

"The LORD bless you!" they called back.

Boaz asked the foreman of his harvesters, "Whose young woman is that?"

The foreman replied, "She is the Moabitess who came back from Moab with
Naomi. She said, 'Please let me glean and gather among the sheaves behind
the harvesters.' She went into the field and has worked steadily from morning till
now, except for a short rest in the shelter."

So Boaz said to Ruth, "My daughter, listen to me. Don't go and glean in
another field and don't go away from here. Stay here with my servant girls.
Watch the field where the men are harvesting, and follow along after the girls. I
have told the men not to touch you. And whenever you are thirsty, go and get a
drink from the water jars the men have filled."

At this, she bowed down with her face to the ground. She exclaimed, "Why
have I found such favor in your eyes that you notice me—a foreigner?"

Boaz replied, "I've been told all about what you have done for your mother-
in-law since the death of your husband—how you left your father and mother
and your homeland and came to live with a people you did not know before.
May the LORD repay you for what you have done. May you be richly rewarded by
the LORD, the God of Israel, under whose wings you have come to take refuge."

"May I continue to find favor in your eyes, my lord," she said. "You have given
me comfort and have spoken kindly to your servant—though I do not have the
standing of one of your servant girls."

At mealtime Boaz said to her, "Come over here. Have some bread and dip it
in the wine vinegar."

Ruth 2:4-14

"Be Ye Kind"

Ephesians 4:32 KJV

WRITE

1 As I read the words on the opposite page my first thought is

_____

_____

2 As I read the words on the opposite page my first feeling is

_____

_____

3 As I think more about the words on the opposite page, the feelings that I have _about myself_ can be described as

_____

_____

_____

SHARE
with the whole group
the thoughts and feelings
that you recorded.

A Word from Norm

Read aloud this "Word from Norm." But first form *three listening teams.* Each team is to listen for and report on one of these questions.

Listening Team #1
Why might some feel frustrated by the command to "be kind"?

Listening Team #2
What are implications of the fact that "kindness" is seen in Scripture as a "fruit of the Spirit"?

Listening Team #3
How do I grow in the character trait of kindness?

(Each team member will find it helpful to take notes.)

Every once in a while we hear the phrase, "getting the cart before the horse." It's a common phrase. And a common experience. We all tend to mix the order of relationships or processes. We get the cart before the horse and are frustrated at our lack of progress.

We've been focusing our attention on this discipleship study on the fruit of the Spirit. Because we're thinking this week, for instance, of "kindness" we will be often tempted to ask, "What can I do to be more kind?" This is good. But there is a danger that in seeking to be kind we miss the secret of true kindness and real goodness. There is a danger we will get the cart before the horse.

You see, kindness, like peace and joy and love, is a by-product. It is an outcome, not an effort. When I seek after the by-product I inevitably become frustrated, because it eludes me. I do not become truly kind until I seek not kindness but the source of kindness. When I find the source, kindness becomes part of my growing character.

Remember what Jesus said? It was not "I will give you the bread of life," but "I *am* the bread of life. He who comes to me will never go hungry" (John 6:35).

When we hunger for kindness in our lives, or for love or joy or peace, we are to discover it in the One who is Joy and who is Love and who is Peace and who is Kindness. The gift is contained in the Giver. The two can never be separated.

The "incomparable riches of His grace, expressed in his kindness to us in Christ Jesus" (Eph. 2:7) is the source of kindness in His people.

We can carry this principle another step. The productivity of my life is rooted in my relationship with God. I cannot grow fruit by myself. Jesus said it clearly in John 15:4: "No branch can bear fruit by itself; it must remain in the vine." Whatever virtues I yearn to see produced in my life will grow through God's life flowing within me, not by my frustrated striving. Many earnest Christians know this truth. But its reality eludes them. Let me suggest several ideas that may prove helpful.

Pursue knowing God. Distinguish between knowing "about" God and knowing Him. As you read Scripture, meditate on what it says about Him and your relationship with Him. For example, Psalm 103:8 says "The Lord is compassionate and gracious, slow to anger, abounding in love." Can you visualize God as compassionate to you? Can you sense Him putting arms around you? Is *your* God compassionate?

Relate His nature to your need. Consider the fruit of the Spirit we've investigated thus far. Do you find yourself lacking in love? In peace? In kindness? Then realize that as you become intimate with Him, His presence will radiate love through you. His closeness will bring peace. His own compassion for others will find expression in your life as kindness.

As a branch, you should not even expect yourself to produce such fruit without Him. Try as hard as you may, such qualities are beyond you and me. But as we remain close to him! Ah, in that transforming relationship Jesus Himself finds room to express His own great love and kindness through you and me.

So let's not get the cart before the horse. Let's not strive to act in kind and loving ways on our own. Instead let's live close to Jesus and then act as His own kindness flows out through our lives.

READ
the Ruth passage again.

What indications are there that Boaz's kindness is rooted in a deep personal relationship with God?

Together find and list below indications of such a relationship.

Just then Boaz arrived from Bethlehem and greeted the harvesters, "The LORD be with you!"

"The LORD bless you!" they called back.

Boaz asked the foreman of his harvesters, "Whose young woman is that?"

The foreman replied, "She is the Moabitess who came back from Moab with Naomi. She said, 'Please let me glean and gather among the sheaves behind the harvesters.' She went into the field and has worked steadily from morning till now, except for a short rest in the shelter."

So Boaz said to Ruth, "My daughter, listen to me. Don't go and glean in another field and don't go away from here. Stay here with my servant girls. Watch the field where the men are harvesting, and follow along after the girls. I have told the men not to touch you. And whenever you are thirsty, go and get a drink from the water jars the men have filled."

At this, she bowed down with her face to the ground. She exclaimed, "Why have I found such favor in your eyes that you notice me—a foreigner?"

Boaz replied, "I've been told all about what you have done for your mother-in-law since the death of your husband—how you left your father and mother and your homeland and came to live with a people you did not know before. May the LORD repay you for what you have done. May you be richly rewarded by the LORD, the God of Israel, under whose wings you have come to take refuge."

Ruth 2:4-12

CONCLUDE

With your partner pray specifically for two individuals to whom you want Christ's own loving-kindness to flow from you this week. Write their names here.

My "overflow" targets

_____

_____

My partner's

_____

_____

THIS WEEK

Pray daily for individuals you listed.

Meditate on the Person of God guided by the verses in your daily journal.

Do meet with or call your partner to share how God has been enriching your life and reaching out to others through you.

PSALM 103

DAY 1

verse 6

DAY 2

verse 8

DAY 3

verse 10

verse 11   **DAY 4**

verse 13   **DAY 5**

verse 17   **DAY 6**

GO ABOUT DOING GOOD 8

"Goodness" seems
such a broad concept.
What does it mean
that Jesus
"went about doing good"
and that we, in Him,
are created
"to do good works"?

READ

this Scripture passage.

The kingdom of heaven is like a landowner who went out early in the morning to hire men to work in his vineyard. He agreed to pay them a denarius for the day and sent them into his vineyard.

About the third hour he went out and saw others standing in the marketplace doing nothing. He told them, "You also go and work in my vineyard, and I will pay you whatever is right." So they went.

He went out again about the sixth hour and the ninth hour and did the same thing. About the eleventh hour he went out and found still others standing around. He asked them, "Why have you been standing there all day long doing nothing?"

"Because no one has hired us," they answered.

He said to them, "You also go and work in my vineyard."

When evening came, the owner of the vineyard said to his foreman, "Call the workers and pay them their wages, beginning with the last ones hired and going on to the first."

The workers who were hired about the eleventh hour came and each received a denarius. So when those came who were hired first, they expected to receive more. But each one of them also received a denarius. When they received it, they began to grumble against the landowner. "These men who were hired last worked only one hour," they said, "and you have made them equal to us who have borne the burden of the work and the heat of the day."

But he answered one of them, "Friend, I am not being unfair to you. Didn't you agree to work for a denarius? Take your pay and go. I want to give the man who was hired last the same as I gave you. Don't I have the right to do what I want with my own money? Or are you envious because I am generous?"

Matthew 20:1-15

DISCUSS

for up to twenty minutes.

1 How would you feel if you were one of the workers hired first?

2 How would you feel if you were one of the workers hired last?

3 Did the workers hired first have a valid basis for complaining?

4 What would happen in our society if employers treated employees this way?

5 Was the landowner fair in his dealings with others? He said he was . . . or did he?

6 What lesson might Jesus have been trying to teach in this story?

7 What does this story have to do with "goodness"?

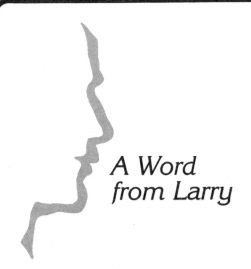

A Word from Larry

There's a real dilemma posed by the story from the Gospel you've just discussed. The landowner did not act with fairness . . . if fairness means treating each one strictly as he deserves.

But then, that is the point of Jesus' story. He's speaking to men who wanted their relationship with God and their reward for serving Him to rest on their own performance. If they were busier for God than others, they felt they deserved more of His blessing.

Jesus' point was that such men had *no right to be upset if God chose to distribute his blessings by another principle!* That principle is seen in the final phrase: "I am generous."

But what does "generosity" have to do with "goodness"? Actually, it is the *same word (agathos)* in the Greek of the New Testament!

This particular word for "good" in the New Testament . . . the word used to describe the "good" fruit of the Spirit . . . was used from earliest times of "good things that evoke a sense of well-being."

Both Testaments link true good with God. The psalmist is sure that "those who seek the Lord lack no good thing" (Ps. 34:10). The New Testament sees no one truly good but God (Matt. 19:17f.) and knows Him as the source and giver of every "good and perfect gift" (James 1:17).

The exciting message of the Bible is that in Christ we have been called to participate in God's own goodness, not simply as recipients, but as givers! And the Bible places a great stress on this high calling. We are to bear fruit in good works (Col. 1:10). We are to seek zealously to do good (1 Thess. 5:15; Titus 3:14). And our good is to be expressed to everyone, not simply those in the household of faith (Gal. 6:6, 10; Rom. 15:2).

But what does "goodness" mean? What is this fruit of the Spirit?

Specifically the word *agathos* means goodness, uprightness, generosity. This is how it happens that the translation of the word *agathos* in the story of the rich landholder becomes the word "generous."

His goodness was expressed in a generous act that did not rest on "fairness" but on a desire for the other's well-being.

Not all "charity" is doing good. But the workers in the vineyard *were* workers. How glad we can be that in rewarding service, God chooses to act out of His generosity rather than strictly by what we deserve.

REFLECT
for a time on your own
experience with God. Then write.

1 How has God shown Himself to be generous with me?

_____

_____

_____

_____

_____

2 How has God's own goodness found expression in my relationships with others?

_____

_____

_____

_____

_____

3 Is there one specific area (or relationship) in which I want to express more of Christ's kind of goodness? If so, what is it?

_____

_____

SHARE

in groups of six
your written answers
from the previous page.

CONCLUDE

Together make a list of *as many* expressions of "doing good" as you can think of that are open to you individually or as a group.

_____

_____

_____

_____

_____

THIS WEEK

Jot down the name of a person you know who demonstrates goodness in his or her life. How does he or she express goodness—actions, attitudes, words?

Study Titus 3 for insights for personal growth in goodness.

_____

PRAY

Save the last few minutes for silent meditation and prayer. Look over the list above, and let God's Spirit show you how He intends to express Jesus' goodness through you this week.

STUDY TITUS 3

DAY 1

DAY 2

DAY 3

DAY 4

DAY 5

DAY 6

93

ENCOURAGE 9

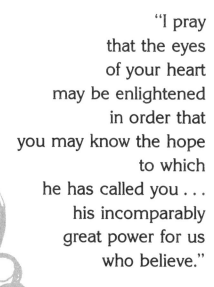

"I pray
that the eyes
of your heart
may be enlightened
in order that
you may know the hope
to which
he has called you . . .
his incomparably
great power for us
who believe."

Ephesians 1:18-19

ENCOURAGEMENT

reflecting, sharing, affirming,
stimulating, *reporting, praying*

What happens when we assemble "to encourage one another"? One of the most significant encouragements we can have is to discover the fact that Christ *is* at work in us and in our brothers and sisters.

Discipleship is not really increased activity on our part. Discipleship involves a more powerful working by God in our lives.

Because we need to keep the focus on what God is doing, and to grow in our confidence in that power of His which is incomparably at work for us who believe, it's important for us to report on His working. And to praise Him in prayer for His commitment to us.

So among the many things that provide us with hope and confidence in God are these. Reporting to each other His good work in us. Praying with each other to praise our wonderful Lord.

And the focus for this Encouragement session?

Reporting. And praise.

IMAGINE

you are
a member of
the church
at Antioch in
New Testament times.

You have sent
Paul and Barnabas
out on
a missionary
journey.

Now they return.

Look at
these verses
from Acts 13.
How important
to you
will their report be?

What benefits
will you personally
receive?

Share your ideas
with the whole
group.

READ

They sailed back to Antioch, where they had been committed to the grace of God for the work they had now completed. On arriving there, they gathered the church together and reported all that God had done through them and how he had opened the door of faith to the Gentiles.

Acts 14:26-27

God Acts

God is at work in us

Philippians 2:13

Report to each other what God
has been doing in your lives
these past weeks. And as each
reports, write down what God
has been doing in the space
at the right and on the next pages.

name
_____
_____
_____
_____
_____
_____
_____
_____
_____
_____
_____
_____
_____
_____

name

name

God is at work in us

Philippians 2:13

name
_____

name
_____

name

name

Praise God!

CONCLUDE

Acts tells of another time of reporting. Peter "explained to them" how salvation first came to the Gentiles.

The response of the church? "When they heard this . . . they praised God" (Acts 11:18).

Conclude your time together now with this same joyful experience. Praise God for His work in your lives!

THIS WEEK

review each day the report of one of your brothers or sisters of God's work in his or her life. As you review, thank and praise the Lord for His work in that life . . . and in your own life.

Make this week a week of praise. And record your thanks in your journal.

STUDY PSALM 100

DAY 1

DAY 2

DAY 3

DAY 4

DAY 5

DAY 6

UNENDING FAITHFULNESS 10

The word "faithful"
is rooted
in that basic word
for saving trust in Christ.
We trust Him
because He is faithful
and trustworthy.
And He is at work
to make us
reliable too!

Trust Reliable

Good faith

Faith

Dependable

Trustworthy Loyal

FAITHFULNESS

Confidence *Faithful*

Assurance

The words to the left
are all words
used in Scripture
to express the
New Testament word
that is translated "faithful"
in Galatians 5:22.

Together
they give us a picture,
first of God,
and then
of the kind of person
He shapes.

Now try to imagine together
the way each person
might live
his or her life.
Be specific in listing
what a "faithful" person
would do.
Also list what such a person
would not do.

a faithful person would . . .

_____

_____

_____

_____

_____

_____

_____

_____

_____

_____

_____

_____

_____

_____

_____

_____

a faithful person would not . . .

_____

_____

_____

_____

_____

_____

_____

_____

_____

_____

_____

_____

_____

_____

_____

_____

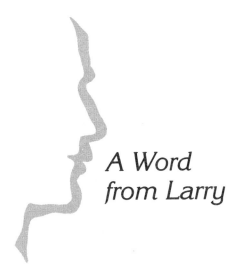

A Word from Larry

The Psalms are a rich source of understanding for us of the confidence that believers, like David, can have in the Lord. And of how our conviction that He is a faithful Person brings to us joy and peace.

To say that God is "faithful" means that no matter what the situation I can have confidence that He will act on my behalf . . . steadfast, faithful, just and compassionate.

One of the psalms which expresses this view of God is the 111th. In it the writer reminds us of all the works of the Lord and invites us to ponder them. As we consider all He has done we see evidence upon evidence that God is indeed one we can trust and extol with all our hearts.

Read this psalm carefully, and underline those indications of His faithfulness which strike you as most significant.

Then, with your partner, work to create a crest, or coat of arms, that will graphically express the faithfulness of God as you understand it.

In creating coats of arms you will of course choose symbols, or pictures, which remind you of or symbolize either acts or characteristics of His faithfulness.

Praise the LORD.

I will extol the LORD with all my heart
  in the council of the upright
  and in the assembly.

Great are the works of the LORD:
  they are pondered by all who delight in them.
Glorious and majestic are his deeds,
  and his righteousness endures forever.
He has caused his wonders to be remembered;
  the LORD is gracious and compassionate.
He provides food for those who fear him;
  he remembers his covenant forever.
He has shown his people the power of his works,
  giving them the lands of other nations.
The works of his hands are faithful and just;
  all his precepts are trustworthy.
They are steadfast for ever and ever,
  done in faithfulness and uprightness.
He provided redemption for his people;
  he ordained his covenant forever—
  holy and awesome is his name.
The fear of the LORD is the beginning of wisdom;
  all who follow his precepts
  have good understanding.
  To him belongs eternal praise.

Psalm 111

"The works
of his hands
are faithful
and just."

Psalm 111:7

CONSIDER

In what ways
would *you* like to be
known as a faithful person?
Make a coat of arms
for yourself,
showing in symbols
or pictures
how you most desire
God to express
the quality of faithfulness
through your own life
and in your own
personal relationships.

"The works of his hands are faithful and just."

Psalm 111:7

SHARE

In groups of six share your coats of arms. Then pray with, and for, each other.

THIS WEEK

As you keep your journal this week, be aware of and record specifically ways that you have had opportunity to express faithfulness in your relationships.

Meditate during the week on Psalm 111, and ask God to shape you more and more into His image as it is expressed there.

And as usual, do share your life this week with your partner and be faithful to pray for him or her.

STUDY PSALM 111

DAY 1

DAY 2

DAY 3

DAY 4

DAY 5

DAY 6

GENTLE AND HUMBLE IN HEART 11

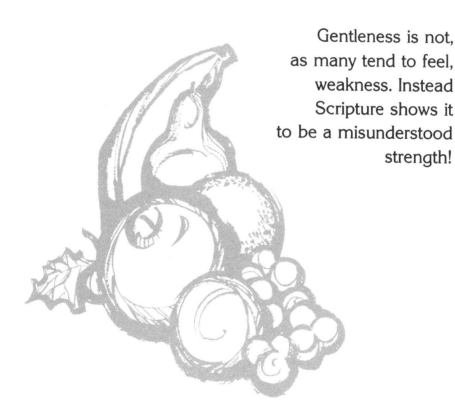

Gentleness is not, as many tend to feel, weakness. Instead Scripture shows it to be a misunderstood strength!

DEFINE

Here are several passages of Scripture in which the same word "gentle" is found as used in Galatians 5.

Examine each passage and jot down your impressions of what "gentle" means in that context.

Study each passage for a minute or two by yourself. Then with the rest of the discipling group share your insights and try together to agree on a definition of what "gentle" really means.

Record the definition you agree on in the sixth square.

Come to me all you who are weary and burdened, and I will give you rest. Take my yoke upon you and learn from me, for I am gentle and humble in heart, and you will find rest for your souls.

Matthew 11:28-29

This took place to fulfill what was spoken through the prophet:

"Say to the Daughter of Zion,
  'See, your king comes to you,
gentle and riding on a donkey,
  on a colt, the foal of a donkey.'"

Matthew 21:5

Therefore, as God's chosen people, holy and dearly loved, clothe yourselves with compassion, kindness, humility, gentleness and patience. Bear with each other and forgive whatever grievances you may have against one another. Forgive as the Lord forgave you.

Colossians 3:12-13

Always be prepared to give an answer to everyone who asks you to give the reason for the hope that you have. But do this with gentleness and respect, keeping a clear conscience, so that those who speak maliciously against your good behavior in Christ may be ashamed of their slander.

1 Peter 3:15-16

The Lord's servant must not quarrel; instead, he must be kind to everyone, able to teach, not resentful. Those who oppose him he must gently instruct, in the hope that God will grant them repentance leading them to a knowledge of the truth.

2 Timothy 2:25

"Gentleness" is _____

_____

_____

_____

_____

_____

_____

_____

A Word from Norm

Read aloud this "Word from Norm" on the contribution of gentleness to relationships.

Look for ways that your combined definition of gentleness is expressed in Norm's thoughts.

Gentleness is a quiet, unassuming quality. We feel its presence without noticing it. It's like a cool breeze on a hot day. Yet, this lovely fruit of the Spirit is powerful in building healthy relationships. What an impact it makes!

Gentleness avoids attitudes which rupture relationships. Proverbs 15:1 reminds us that the gentle answer turns away wrath. Gentleness defuses the angry person. Several years ago, a friend told me of a study he knew about in which supervisors were taught to reply in a gentle manner to irate workers. The results were reduced tension and disputes.

Gentleness disarms the opponent who wants to push against me. He finds that I do not choose to build walls of resistance; I have no need to threaten him, get tough, fight back. My kind, humble attitude does not foster hostility.

The gentle person builds up others. His gentleness provides strength for a healthy relationship. A part of the reason is gentle actions are built on the attitude of meekness. To many people meekness carries the idea of weakness or frailty. This is never true biblically. Meekness is an inner grace planted by the Spirit. It expresses itself as an unusual strength of character. The truly meek person has a Spirit-given peace which frees him to act gently.

The gentle person provides rest for the weary. Jesus said, "I am gentle and humble in heart, and you will find rest for your souls" (Matt. 11:29). When the Spirit is able to produce gentleness in us it will attract others who are weary, seeking a quiet refuge.

The gentle person also nurtures others. The apostle Paul described his relationship with the Thessalonian Christians like the gentle mother who tenderly nurtures her infant (1 Thess. 2:7). The quiet and peaceful spirit nourishes the soul, encourages growth. Seeds that are sown in this soil bear fruit.

While gentleness describes a person it also describes a relationship. It pictures how I act toward another person. I approach the other in a spirit of peace, bringing the aroma of good will. My quiet actions create the spirit of harmony.

When I am indwelt by the spirit of gentleness my own life is enriched. I enjoy more harmonious relationships with others. God's indwelling peace allows me to approach uncertain and stressful situations without anxiety. In the strength of meekness I can act with gentleness. I am able to be a better steward of my energy because I do not dissipate it with anxiety, strife or frustration.

Gentleness is my friend.

Discuss

Look at these typical situations, and discuss in depth how a person who is gentle might react or respond in each one. Be thorough in your descriptions. In the process, apply what you have learned from your Bible study of gentleness. Look at each case from the point of view of the person who is "offended."

1 In an important discussion another person angrily disagrees.

2 In the home an older child reacts angrily to a parent's request.

3 A teenager's brother calls her a name.

4 At work a co-worker is found to be telling lies to beat another out of a promotion.

5 A couple dispute over "submission."

SHARE

If you have situations in your own relationships in which you would like help in better understanding a "gentle" response, briefly write about it here. Then share—either with the whole group or in smaller clusters of four or six.

_____

_____

_____

_____

_____

_____

CLOSE

Conclude with prayer, focusing on the situations any in the group may have shared which involve them.

THIS WEEK

Reread "A Word from Norm." Underline sentences or phrases which challenge you to growth in gentleness. Beside each underlined statement jot down one specific way you could act on it.

JOURNAL

MEDITATE ON HEBREWS 4:14–5:2

DAY 1

DAY 2

DAY 3

DAY 4

DAY 5

DAY 6

ADD SELF CONTROL 12

How frustrating it is
to lack self-control!
And yet many of us
have grown up
without knowing
how to discipline
ourselves
to reach goals.
So this
fruit of the Spirit
is truly important
to many of us
as followers of
the Lord.

ANALYZE

Here is an important Bible passage that deals with the issue of self-control.

Read the passage. Then on the following pages trace the analysis of the passage.

Sample notes are included on the first page. On the next pages work together as a group to gain your own insights and make your own observations.

The passage will help build confidence that self-control *is* one of the gifts God gives to those who choose to follow Jesus.

His divine power has given us everything we need for life and godliness through our knowledge of him who called us by his own glory and goodness. Through these he has given us his very great and precious promises, so that through them you may participate in the divine nature and escape the corruption in the world caused by evil desires.

For this very reason, make every effort to add to your faith goodness; and to goodness, knowledge; and to knowledge, self-control; and to self-control, perseverance; and to perseverance, godliness; and to godliness, brotherly kindness; and to brotherly kindness, love. For if you possess these qualities in increasing measure, they will keep you from being ineffective and unproductive in your knowledge of our Lord Jesus Christ. But if anyone does not have them, he is nearsighted and blind, and has forgotten that he has been cleansed from his past sins.

2 Peter 1:3-9

His divine power _God's unlimited ability_ is the
source of my expectation of self control.

has given us everything we need for life and godliness
It is mine now. I only need to use it.

through our knowledge of him who called us _I'll find_
it in Him and knowing Him ... not in
self - effort.

by his own glory and goodness.

He has given us his very great and precious promises._____

_____

_____

through them you may participate in the divine nature_____

_____

_____

and escape the corruption in the world caused by evil desires.___

_____

_____

For this reason, make every effort to add to your faith goodness;

_____

_____

to goodness, knowledge; to knowledge, self-control; _____

_____

_____

to self-control, perseverance . . . _____

_____

_____

For if you possess these qualities in increasing measure, they will keep you from being ineffective and unproductive in your knowledge of our Lord Jesus Christ.

_____

_____

_____

A Word from Norm

Life for many people is like an ocean: the mire of failure is constantly being stirred up. Instability controls them like unseen currents. Crashing waves break up the little order they have. For such individuals the hope of self-control is a vanishing dream.

God's Word speaks of self-control as a reality for us. The word *enkrateia* contains the idea of strength, mastery, power, self-control. The word is used in 1 Corinthians 9:25 to describe the athlete disciplining his body to achieve a goal.

But what about you and me? Have we discovered the Spirit's fruit of self-control? Is He leading us to growth? Is His power liberating us from defeat? Is His power enabling us to find self-control?

The following questions help us probe this issue. They reflect my side of the human-Spirit relationship.

Am I committed to order in my life? Observe two people: One has a sense of personal order. He plans his day. When interruptions occur he can cope with them and not lose direction. The other person flits from one activity to another, getting sidetracked by distractions, and leaves a trail of unfinished intentions.

Do I plan to achieve my goals? When I taught in graduate school I observed well-educated students who waited until the day before a term paper was due to work on it. As I discussed the problem with them I noted that they seldom had a study plan. They waited until the deadline became alarmingly close and then worked frantically to complete the task. Rarely did they achieve their true potential. Wise planning would have helped them immensely.

Think about this!

Do you *plan* to arrive at meetings late?

Do you *plan* not to do those tasks that are unfinished?

Do you *plan* not to spend time with your spouse/children?

Now jot down an area where you would like better self-control.

Do I set priorities? Frequently individuals do not have mastery over their lives because they have not set priorities. What is most important for me to accomplish today? Is it important enough that I'll push other activities, or distractions, away to focus my energies on this priority?

Do I REALLY want self-control? Perhaps what I call lack of self-control is actually an unwillingness to face a problem. Perhaps it is *something I don't want to control.* (If I've never *really* decided I'm going to get up on time, though I say I should, even my plans will fall through because I am not genuinely committed.)

God wants to give us order and stability in our lives. His power is available for that purpose. He calls us to commit ourselves to growth in areas where the lack of self-control exists.

My Plan of Action

Commitment has direction.

1 Jot down one *specific* area of life in which you desire greater self-control.

   _____

2 List three *specific* actions you can take to develop greater self-control in that area.

   _____

   _____

   _____

3 Share your plan of action with your partner. Let him or her offer suggestions and jot them down below. Commit yourselves to pray daily for each other.

   _____

   _____

   _____

THIS WEEK

Record daily how you are following your "action plan." This week's
Scripture (1 Peter 1:3–9) will encourage you as you venture into new
areas of self-control. And be sure again to meet with or phone your
partner, to share what is happening and pray for each other.

JOURNAL

STUDY 2 PETER 1:3-9

DAY 1

DAY 2

DAY 3

DAY 4

DAY 5

DAY 6

137

ENCOURAGE 13

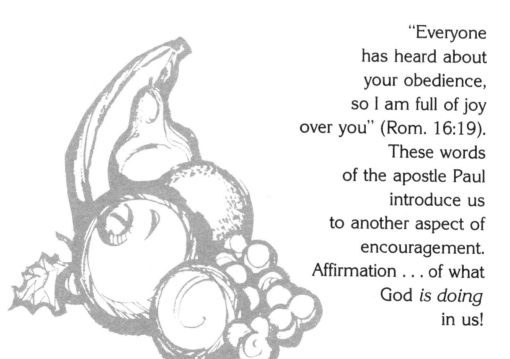

"Everyone
has heard about
your obedience,
so I am full of joy
over you" (Rom. 16:19).
These words
of the apostle Paul
introduce us
to another aspect of
encouragement.
Affirmation . . . of what
God *is doing*
in us!

ENCOURAGEMENT
reflecting, sharing, *affirming,*
stimulating, reporting, praying

In this discipling process you have shared many vital experiences. You've looked into Scripture. You've looked into each other's lives. You've stood with each other in prayer. You've seen God work, and praised Him. Now at the end of this study of the fruit of the Spirit, there is one more encouraging experience.

We see it often in Scripture. "I thank God I can have complete confidence in you," Paul says to the Corinthians. "I have no one likeminded," Paul compliments Timothy.

Recognizing God's work in our brother or sister . . . and telling them what we see . . . is one of the good ways that God has given us to encourage each other.

And to praise Him.

Affirm

to tell others the positive
strengths, growth, and progress
we see in their lives.

STRENGTHS

Write down
the names
of those
who are with you
in this
discipling study.

By each one
write down
his or her
strengths.

When you have
all finished
this listing,
turn together
to the next page.

NAME _____

STRENGTHS _____

_____

_____

_____

_____

_____

_____

_____

_____

_____

_____

_____

_____

_____

_____

_____

NAME   STRENGTHS

"Now unto Him
who is able to
do . . . to Him
be glory in the
Church and in
Christ Jesus
throughout all
generations, for
ever and ever!
Amen!"

Ephesians 3:20-21

SHARE

Spend this Encouragement session sharing with each person the strengths you have observed, which God has worked in each personality. It may be good to form a circle, have one member sit in the center, and let all the others share the good things they see in him or her. This is *affirming*.

RECORD

When it is your turn, be sure to remember and record here what your brethren have seen of God's work in you. Accept their testimony . . . and review it each day this week as a basis for personal praise to God.

_____

_____

_____

_____

_____

_____

_____

_____

_____

_____